# PRAYER
## Common Sense
## and the Bible

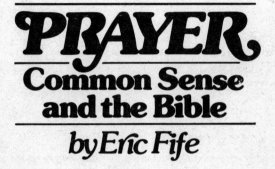

# PRAYER
## Common Sense and the Bible

*by Eric Fife*

# ZONDERVAN
## PUBLISHING HOUSE

OF THE ZONDERVAN CORPORATION
GRAND RAPIDS, MICHIGAN 49506

Prayer Common Sense and the Bible
Copyright © 1976 by The Zondervan Corporation
Grand Rapids, Michigan

**Library of Congress Cataloging in Publication Data**

Fife, Eric S
    Prayer.

    1. Prayer.    I. Title.
BV210.2.F5      248'.3      76-43017

We are grateful to the following publishers for permission to use
their Bible translations in our book.

*The New English Bible.* Copyright © 1961 and 1970 by The Dele-
gates of the Oxford University Press and The Syndics of the Cam-
bridge University Press.

*The New Testament in Modern English* by J. B. Phillips. Copyright
© 1958, 1960, 1972 by J. B. Phillips. Printed by The Macmillan
Company.

*The Revised Standard Version.* Copyright © 1946, 1952 and 1972
by Division of Christian Education of the National Council of the
Churches of Christ in the United States of America.

Third printing   January 1978
ISBN 0-310-24332-7
*Printed in the United States of America*

to JOAN and JANET —
my wife and daughter
who made this book possible

# Contents

# Foreword

Prayer may well hold the distinction of being the most talked about and least practiced aspect of the Christian life. Every Christian pays lip service to the importance of prayer but most of us, if we are honest, must confess that our practice falls far short of our preaching.

There are many reasons for this. One is expressed in that oft-quoted sentence:

Satan trembles when he sees
The weakest saint upon his knees.

Therefore, Satan will do all he can to keep Christians from prayer. Other reasons include such things as the needed discipline for prayer (which most of us find difficult to exercise), the fact that prayer is hard work (which most of us shun), the problems of unanswered prayer (which most of us prefer to hide), and misunderstandings about what prayer really is — to mention just a few.

Eric Fife has struggled with these problems in his own life. Long years of ministry in the pastorate in England and the U.S., in student work with Inter-Varsity Christian Fellowship, as well as in mission leadership with the North Africa Mission, have given him a practical as well as a biblical perspective on this issue. He has observed the practice, the problems, and the results of prayer in the Bible, in his own life, and in the lives of others. He has struggled in prayer with new believers, with students, and with more mature Christians. He has purposely held off writing on this topic, even though he studied it and preached on it for many years, because he felt the need for this perspective. Mr. Fife now brings to us the results of study, observation, and practice. Much of what he says will not sound new to some, but he has "put the cookies on the lower shelf" where even the youngest Christian may find them and where all may enjoy them.

Prayer is seen in its broad scope as not being limited to the super saints nor restricted by narrow guidelines. It is seen rather as that indispensable link between every believer and our Lord to be enjoyed in its fullness and not stifled by restrictive concepts of the "what" or "hows" of its use. There is a liberating freshness in this book which should motivate the reader to a more enjoyable prayer life.

I commend this book for its biblical foundations, its practical insights, and its balanced motivation in leading us to the Lord.

*David M. Howard*

# Introduction

It began when I lived in Winchester, which was the ancient capital of England long before the Norman conquest. As a young pastor I had some deep problems concerning prayer in my own life, and also in my ministry. I collected what books I could upon the subject, but the more I studied them the more frustrated I became. The experience of others often seemed not to apply to my own prayers. At times I wondered if my praying was worthwhile. Sometimes I wondered if those who wrote on prayer were just "super saints" or if they were silent regarding failure. I wondered if they attempted a sincere but wrong effort to save the reputation of God!

After I had been a Christian for about ten years I became strongly influenced by Dr. D. Martyn Lloyd-Jones, then the minister of Westminster Chapel. He was then leading weekly Bible discussion which I attended. The subjects were varied but one emphasis was unvaried. Many subjects were questioned. Was it taught by God in the Scriptures or was it merely the tradition of men. I have tried ever since to apply that principle. In honesty I must warn that such an approach does not make for a quiet life or for popularity.

Eventually I took a step, that in retrospect seems to be bold. I made a list of questions about prayer to which I had no answers. I had the questions printed and announced to my congregation that I would be preaching on them. I put away all my books about prayer and resolved to look in the Bible alone for the answers. I spent much time in study and prayer and often tramped the countryside to help clear my mind. I preached the sermons — I still have some of the original notes. People seemed to be helped by the sermons but the greatest blessing was to myself.

Later I was engaged for many years in ministry to students and found that many of them had similar questions to those I had faced. To know that such questions were genuine often seemed to give a sense of relief and many expressed their appreciation for help received.

A book such as this would have saved me much heartache and confusion when I was younger and I hope that it will be of some help to others now. I have not expressed these views in writing before because I am conscious of the discrepancy between teaching and practice. I have spent many years preaching and thinking about prayer, but I still find myself in the position of the disciples when they asked, "Lord, teach us to pray."

# 1 Twisting God's Arm

A high school senior said to me recently, "I have just come to realize that ever since I became a Christian I have looked upon prayer as a means of persuading God to do what I want Him to do — a kind of religious arm-twisting."

He had put his finger on a fatal flaw not only in his prayer life, but also in that of many Christians. He had made more progress than most of us, because he had come to see his mistake. Most do not.

Many churches and Christian groups try to collect prayers with much the same zeal politicians collect signatures on a petition. The idea seems to be the more people, the more prayers, the greater the blessing. This suggests that God is influenced mainly by the arithmetic of prayer. This is not much different from the Buddhist who writes out a prayer, fastens it to a wheel, and then keeps the wheel spinning as fast as he can for as long as he can, believing that the more it spins, the greater will be the response from God.

Some Buddhists fix their wheels so that the wind will keep them turning even while they are asleep. If our God were that kind of God think what possibilities there would be for us with the internal combustion engine, or better yet the turbine! Of course we know that God is not like that, and that such a view is nothing like the one we should have on prayer.

It is natural for most of us to want to measure or compare everything because we are raised in that kind of world. The businessman thinks about his balance sheet and his bank account, the teacher about his or her students in terms of their grades, and the car buff in terms of horsepower and r.p.ms. It is not surprising then that we do much the same with prayer.

How many people attended the prayer meeting?

How many of them prayed?

How long did they pray?

It is because we have such a passion for statistics that we talk as if the number of people at the prayer meeting determines the success of the church program. This is no new mistake. Jesus had a name for it — "for they think they will be heard for their many words" (Matt. 6:7, RSV).

God is concerned about how seriously we take the matter of prayer — and that includes our attitude to the prayer meeting — but He is not a God of arithmetic. It is important that we develop our ideas about prayer carefully. We must know what prayer is as well as what it is not.

So, what is prayer? Perhaps the best description of prayer at its simplest is the one given by O. Hallesby. He begins by discussing the difference between air and breath. Air is around us at all times. In fact, it exerts a pressure upon our bodies of 14.7 lbs. per square inch. However much we may be surrounded by air, it never becomes breath until we admit it to our lungs by inhaling. As with air, God is with us and surrounds us at all times. When we take the initiative to admit His presence into our minds, it is prayer. Prayer is simply letting God in. It is allowing Him to fill our beings. It is not presenting a shopping list to God; it is two-way communication. The Lord said, "Behold, I stand at the door and knock; if anyone hears my voice and opens the door, I will come in to him and eat with him, and he with me" (Rev. 3:20, RSV).

In a family relationship it may be appropriate for a son to give his father a Christmas gift list, but we would think it to be a poor relationship if it was the only relationship between father and son. If the only view a son has of his father is that of a year-round Santa Claus it is a pathetic relationship and is bankrupt of true family affection. But this is similar to the view many of us have of God and of prayer. It is much like that of the little girl who one night told her mother she didn't need to say her prayers because she didn't want anything.

Prayer is a two-way communication with God. True communication between friends means listening as well as talking. It means learning about each other and enjoying each other's company. We feel we have had a poor evening if one person dominates the entire conversation. Prayer is not nonstop talking. Paul told us to "pray constantly" (1 Thess. 5:17, RSV). He obviously did not mean nonstop talking. We would have time for nothing else. Surely what he meant was that we must simply relate every situation in life to God and admit Him into everything we do just as we admit air into our lungs.

There are times when we are very conscious of breathing. When we first learn to scuba dive we are aware of every breath we take. Most of the time, however, we do not think about breathing at all; it becomes a natural function. So it is with prayer. We may be aware of it at first, and perhaps may even be self-conscious about it, but we should cultivate the habit of relating every detail of our lives to God and admit Him to every circumstance. This is prayer at its simplest. There is far more to prayer than this, but this is the place to start.

It would be a strange situation if a couple were engaged to be married and yet never wanted to spend time in each other's company. We would consider this a poor prospect for a happy marriage. Similarly, there is something wrong if we have no desire to spend time with God, to get to know Him better, to listen to what He has to teach us about Himself.

It is as bad to ignore God as it is to simply regard Him as a year-round Santa Claus. One of the most remarkable things we learn about God is that He actually wants our fellowship and has made it possible for us to have a living, honest relationship with Him. If He truly is our father and we are His children, we shall want to be with Him and to enjoy Him. This is prayer.

True prayer does not make God the target of a barrage of words, the object of our neglect, or a perpetual Santa Claus. It makes Him the center of our affection and our partner in fellowship.

Prayer involves *listening* to God as well as *talking* to Him. This can best be accomplished by reading the Scriptures. It is not always recognized that Scripture reading is a form of prayer, but it is. It gives the Lord the opportunity to speak to us.

* * *

It is right to make our needs known to God (although it is good to remember He knows them already), but since prayer is fellowship with someone we love, we should be sure that we devote adequate attention to telling Him about our love and affection for Him. Be certain that prayer is not an exercise in armtwisting but is two-way communication with someone we love.

17

# 2 Prayers That Bounce

Have you ever had a check bounce? Do you have any idea how many checks bounce each year? Every bank has its conditions before a check can be cashed. Many people know this, but few Christians seem aware that God has laid down conditions that must be fulfilled before our prayers will be honored. Many prayers that are prayed simply bounce and we wonder why God does not answer them.

God has good reasons for making conditions before He answers prayer. Prayer is a tremendous power and it must be safeguarded. Just as a pistol has a safety catch and a hydrogen bomb has a fail-safe mechanism, so prayer must not be left in irresponsible hands. People have been made alive and have been killed by prayer, so God sets the conditions.

We have all heard much about the promises

of prayer, such as, "Ask whatever you will, and it shall be done for you" (John 15:7, RSV), and "If two of you agree on earth about anything they ask, it will be done for them" (Matt. 18:19, RSV). However, we rarely hear about the conditions that must be fulfilled before prayers are truly effective. There are at least six in the New Testament, and each one is connected with the other.

### FAITH

"Let him ask in faith, nothing wavering. For he that wavereth is like a wave of the sea driven with the wind and tossed. For let not that man think that he shall receive any thing from the Lord" (James 1:7, KJV).

Why is faith so important in our praying? Because prayer is not just getting things from God, but is intimate companionship between two persons. When a husband and wife do not trust each other, there is no true harmony and fellowship. Prayer in its best sense is harmony with God, and harmony is not found if there is doubt and suspicion.

How do we develop this faith if we do not possess it? Many people seem to imagine that faith is related mainly to emotion. They *feel* faith in God or in someone else. This often leads to all kinds of gimmicks to "get into the right mood," such as certain types of music or tones of voice. This is not only useless, but is also dangerous because it can lead people to think they are praying effectively when all they are doing is developing a warm glow inside. Faith is not feeling.

Faith is not a mood. It is connected far more with the intellect and the will than with the emotions. It is not feeling good that makes you go off the high diving board; it is will power. The way to strengthen our faith is not to concentrate on the circumstances, like Peter when he walked upon the water.

"Faith comes from what is heard, but what is heard comes from the preaching of Christ" (Rom. 10:17, RSV). There is no shortcut. When we learn more about God, we trust Him more. Faith is like a muscle; the more we use it, the stronger it becomes.

## A RIGHT MOTIVE

It is possible to do the wrong thing for the wrong reason. "You ask and do not receive, because you ask wrongly, to spend it on your passions" (James 4:3, RSV).

The way to strengthen our faith is to concentrate on God and His Word. Even when we pray, we must be sure that our prayer does not spring from a selfish motive or we shall not fulfill the second condition of successful prayer.

## KNOWING THE WILL OF GOD

In some ways I find this the most difficult condition of all. I remember as a young pastor being called to the home of one of my members whose son was in convulsions. "God will make him better, won't He?" asked the anxious mother. "He certainly can do so," I replied. This did not satisfy the mother. "Yes, I know He can, but will He?" she asked. To this I had no answer.

"And this is the confidence which we have in him, that if we ask anything according to his will he hears us" (1 John, 5:14, RSV). But what is according to His will? That is really the snag, and is probably the reason why so many of our prayers bounce. Prayer is not a blank check so that we can get what we want. To pray according to the will of God means that we have to know what that will is, and that is not easy for most of us. Our problem is not, "Can God answer this prayer?" but "Does God want to answer it?" "We know not what to pray for as we ought," says Paul. We know only a small part of the situation. Only He knows it all. This is where the snag comes in. Many of us do not live near enough to Him to know His will.

There are a few people, however, who seem to get amazing answers to prayer. Hudson Taylor was one and George Mueller was another. Why is this? In 1 Corinthians 12:9 Paul suggests that some Christians are given a special gift of faith, and I believe that this is what is meant. In a particular situation they have a special knowledge of the will of God.

This also brings us to the fourth condition of prayer.

"If you abide in me, and my words abide in you, ask whatever you will, and it shall be done for you" (John 15:7, RSV). If we are living that close to Jesus we are not likely to ask for things He does not want us to have. Phillips translates the verse, "if you live your life in me, and my words live in your hearts, you can ask for whatever you like and it will come true."

The chapter from which these quotes were taken makes it clear that the Christian should be as connected with Jesus as the branch is to the vine. You cannot get a closer contact than that. That means letting ourselves be saturated by the Lord and His Word. Then we shall "pray according to his will."

The next condition is connected with the ones before it.

### A PURE HEART

We cannot live in fellowship with God and know His will if there is sin in our lives. "If I regard iniquity in my heart, the Lord will not hear me" (KJV), said the psalmist in Psalm 66:18, and there are many other places where God expresses similar ideas.

No Christian can live without sin, but he can remain in fellowship with God only by confessing that sin and being forgiven. An important part of a healthy prayer life is asking forgiveness, and that makes it possible to live in fellowship with God. One of the most difficult phrases in the English language is "I was wrong." Another is "I am sorry." They are part of the vocabulary of the Christian who has an effective prayer life.

## A FORGIVING SPIRIT

This is really a part of the previous point. Jesus said, "Whenever you stand praying, forgive, if you have anything against anyone" (Mark 11:25, RSV). Many prayers bounce off the ceiling because we do not forgive people. We may be in the right, and so was Jesus, but He asked that His persecutors be forgiven, even when He hung upon the cross.

An unforgiving spirit not only ruins our fellowship with another person, but also with God. That is clear from 1 John 2:9: "One who hates his brother is in darkness."

\*     \*     \*

A banker told me recently that every year in the United States thousands of checks bounce. I'm afraid that this is true also of prayers. Let us make sure it is not true of our prayers.

# 3 Variety: The Spice of Prayer Life

Few things are more maddening than listening to a person hitting one note on a piano again and again. If we are ever to produce true music, it is important to learn all the notes. Many Christians have learned only one or two elementary facts about prayer, and therefore their prayer life is stagnant and boring.

Christians are slow to learn that there are various forms of prayer, and some never get beyond the "shopping list" type of prayer. There are at least seven types of prayer that God meant us to use and we will consider these in this chapter. If we do not use the variety of prayer that is taught in the Bible we will never be enriched as God intended.

### ONE: THANKSGIVING

Appreciation is basic to every relationship.

It is a poor marriage in which the husband never expresses appreciation for the work of his wife in the home. This is true also in the relationship between God and man. "It is a good thing to give thanks to the LORD" says the psalmist in Psalm 92:1, and that theme is echoed throughout the Bible in such references as Ephesians 5:20; Philippians 4:6; Colossians 3:17; and 1 Thessalonians 5:18, in which Paul tells us to give thanks in all circumstances.

To be strong and stable, our prayer life should have a good foundation of thanksgiving. This means developing an attitude of thanksgiving, as well as a vocabulary. If when praying for a person you pray only for his faults to be corrected, you develop a negative outlook, but if you make a point of thanking God for that person's strengths you will be praying in a scriptural manner and will be likely to avoid having a critical spirit. Notice in the letters of Paul how frequently he mentions that he gives thanks to God for those to whom he is writing.

### TWO: PRAISE AND ADORATION

Praise, adoration, and worship are virtually the same and often are confused with thanksgiving, but there is an important difference between them. A wife likes to be appreciated for what she does, but even more she needs to be loved for who she is. Her husband needs to express that love. We thank God for what He gives; we praise Him for who He is.

For most people praise is the weakest part of their prayer life. This is because it probably is the most difficult to do. One reason we find it difficult to praise the Lord is because we devote so little time and effort to understanding how wonderful He is. This failure is not merely that of the individual Christian, but also that of the church and its ministers.

We seldom hear sermons that describe the character and attributes of God, and there are several reasons for this. God is so much greater than anything or anyone, that it is difficult even to begin to study His greatness. In past centuries great men of God have given much attention to God's attributes but for the most part our modern minds find their writing involved and dull. A more recent writer has tried to correct this deficiency. *The Knowledge of the Holy* by the late A. W. Tozer is devoted to this theme and the book will repay careful and repeated study. If you have a good hymnal the sections containing hymns on the Attributes of God and on the Life of Jesus Christ will be a wonderful seam to be mined.

Another problem in the matter of praise and worship is that of the means of expression. Even if we have an adequate understanding of the Lord we usually lack the ability to express it. This is not surprising. As the hymn writer wrote, if we

> Join all the glorious names
> Of wisdom, love, and power,

All are too mean to speak His worth,
Too mean to set my Saviour forth.

The English language is one of the richest and most expressive known to man, but it still is inadequate to do justice to the character and attributes of God.

Although praise and worship are often neglected in prayer, they are most important. In John 4:23 Jesus makes it clear that the Father seeks people "who will worship the Father in spirit and in truth." In his first letter Peter stresses the fact that Christians are to be "a holy priesthood, to offer spiritual sacrifices acceptable to God" and that we should "declare the wonderful deeds of him who has called you out of darkness into His marvelous light" (1 Peter 2:5,9, RSV). It is not by chance that the first characteristic of the new-born Church at Pentecost was that "we hear them telling in our own tongues the mighty works of God" (Acts 2:11, RSV).

We must praise and worship God because He wants us to, and also because He deserves more than we can ever offer. Praise is also a great means of blessing to the individual because it is a great cure for pride and for depression, as it turns our attention away from ourselves and to the Lord.

If praise is difficult how can we learn to develop its practice? Fortunately we are not without help.

If our vocabulary is inadequate there are

many other men of God who have expressed their worship and adoration in forms we can use. It is a good idea to write on to the back flyleaf of your Bible a list of suitable passages of Scripture. Some of these are Exodus 15:1-18; 1 Samuel 2:1-11; 1 Chronicles 16:8-36; 29:9-15; Psalms 66; 67; 86; 93; 95; 96; 97; 98; 99; 103; 111; 113; 146; 149; 150; Revelation 15:3,4. I have found that it is invaluable to memorize some of these.

All good hymnals have a wide range of hymns that can be read or sung as an act of worship and praise. Usually these are grouped under several categories in the Table of Contents, such as:

> God the Father
> His Attributes
> God in Nature
> Adoration
> Jesus Christ
> Life and Ministry
> Ascension
> His Coming in Glory
> Worship and Praise

Actually many people find it easy to memorize hymns of worship because of the rhythm and rhyme, and I think more of these great hymns should be used in our churches and homes. I have spent many hours driving on the freeways and highways worshiping God by singing the hymns of praise I have memorized.

It would be good for us to cultivate the ability of praising the Lord in our own words as well as with those written by others. We may not be eloquent, but the Lord looks into our hearts and it will be like spiritual music to Him.

How good it is to be with a group of people who have really learned to worship, and to spend a special period of the prayer meeting in adoration of our God by using some or all of the methods I have mentioned.

It is important to remember also, that no matter how busy we are in work for God, and whatever sacrifice we make, it will be inadequate unless we "continually offer up a sacrifice of praise to God, that is, the fruit of lips that acknowledge his name" (Heb. 13:15, RSV).

### THREE: INTERCESSION

The Bible teaches us that as Christians we are priests. "Him who loves us . . . and made us . . . priests to his God and Father" (Rev. 1:5,6, RSV), and we are "a royal priesthood" (1 Peter 2:5, RSV). This is not the place to examine all that is meant by the fact that we are priests, but it does remind us that one of the functions of a priest is to pray on behalf of others — and what a privilege this is.

We find many examples of prayers of intercession in the New Testament. The best example is set by Christ Himself in His great prayer that fills John 17. Paul also gives us many examples in almost all his letters. One such prayer is found in Ephesians 3:14-19.

Not only are there examples of how to pray for others, but we also have requests to do so. "I appeal to you, brethren, by our Lord Jesus Christ and by the love of the Spirit, to strive together with me in your prayers to God on my behalf" (Rom. 15:30, RSV). "Brethren, pray for us" (1 Thess. 5:25, RSV). "Keep alert with all perseverance, making supplication for all the saints" (Eph. 6:18, RSV).

It is clear then that a part of our prayer time will be intercession, and for some it may occupy the largest part of their prayer time. In 1 Corinthians 12:9, in a section on the gifts of the spirit, Paul refers "to another faith by the same Spirit" (RSV). This obviously does not refer to "saving faith." I often have thought that this may refer to some who have a special ministry of intercession. I have never received that particular gift but I have known many who have. It is clear that intercession must be an indispensable ingredient in the life of every Christian.

### FOUR: PETITION

Petition is simply the part of our prayer life where we make known our needs to God. Probably this is the type of prayer about which we need least urging or advice; however, there are one or two important things to remember.

In chapter 2 we considered the preconditions for effective prayer. We shall need to act on these requirements in reminding God of our needs. In praying for ourselves it is important to remember the examples of prayers of our Lord and the apostle Paul. We notice that their emphasis was upon spiritual needs rather than material needs. At the same time it is encouraging, and even inspiring, to know that not one detail of our lives is too insignificant to our Father. "Do not be anxious, saying, 'What shall we eat?' or 'What shall we drink?' or 'What shall we wear?' . . . your heavenly Father knows that you need them all" (Matt. 6:31,32, RSV).

A good father takes an interest in his children's hobbies, their homework, and their friends. God is that kind of Father. Many good human fathers have concern for their children but insufficient time; our heavenly Father has both unlimited concern and infinite time for His children.

### FIVE: REPENTANCE

Not many of us enjoy apologizing or admitting we are wrong. Obviously we have too much pride and it is shown in the lack of repentance in our relationships with God and people. "The higher a man grows in grace the lower he falls in his own estimation," said Charles H. Spurgeon. A small view of God leads to an inflated idea of ourselves.

Paul was a spiritual giant but his life was full of repentance and brokenness. "I am content with weaknesses, insults, hardships, persecutions, and calamities; for when I am weak, then I am strong" (2 Cor. 12:10, RSV), "Not that we are sufficient of ourselves" (2 Cor. 3:5, KJV). "Wretched man that I am! Who will deliver me from this body of death?" (Rom. 7:24, RSV).

32

Paul never cringed before men or in the face of duty. He was no pathetic Uriah Heep. Once he saw the glory of Jesus Christ during that journey to Damascus, he fell on his face and metaphorically never got up again. He was mighty before men because he was broken before God.

If we compare the life of King Saul with that of King David we may well conclude that David was as much a sinner as Saul, and perhaps even more so. The significant difference between them is the willingness of David to accept reproof. e.g. "David said to Nathan, 'I have sinned against the LORD'" (2 Sam. 12:13, RSV). The fifty-first Psalm is probably the greatest outpouring of repentance known in history. This quality of David is surely one of the reasons why he is called "a man after God's own heart." Another such example of repentance is found in Ezra 9 and 10.

Penitential prayer has become unfashionable, but penitence always has figured largely in the history of the church. This was confirmed by its place in the seventeenth-century prayer book. It often appears in the writing of puritans and mystics. Repentance was often upon the lips of martyrs as they marched to their death.

I believe there are two main causes for this phenomenon. The first has been mentioned, and it is the small view we have of God. I suspect the second cause is a completely wrong idea of what repentance is.

Much confusion is caused because many

think that repentance is a matter of emotion. It is more a matter of the will. God does not say "If you *feel* sorry I will forgive you! He says, "If we confess our sins, he . . . will forgive our sins and cleanse us." (1 John 1:9, RSV). I once knew a man who had a remarkably close relationship with God. Whenever there was a cloud in his relationship with God, he would confess without fuss and go on his happy way. His wife was a more reserved person, and one day she remarked to her husband. "Ed, you deal with your sin with so little fuss, it is hardly decent." She had made the mistake of thinking that true repentance means being emotionally depressed by guilt. This morbid depression originates in man rather than God. We need to examine ourselves for sin for only as long as it takes to recognize it and confess it. Then we may immediately enjoy forgiveness and fellowship with God.

There are private sins that require private repentance, and there are sins against one person that require an apology to that individual. There also are public sins that require public confession. Generally the scope of the sin will set the scope of the confession.

### SIX: CONTEMPLATION OF NATURE

It has long puzzled me why Christians neglect nature as a means of communion with God. We sing in the words of George Wade Robinson,

> Heav'n above is softer blue,
> Earth around is sweeter green;

> Something lives in every hue
> Christless eyes have never seen.

But is it really true in our own experience?

Paul wrote, "His invisible nature, namely, his eternal power and deity, has been clearly perceived in the things that have been made" (Rom. 1:20, RSV). When David watched the stars in the night skies he saw the glory of God which is so beautifully expressed in Psalm 8, especially in verses 3 and 9. "When I look at thy heavens, the work of thy fingers, the moon and the stars which thou established," and "how majestic is thy name in all the earth!" (RSV). When David watched the glory of the heavens in daylight he saw the reflections of the glory of God. "The heavens are telling the glory of God; and the firmament proclaims his handiwork" (Ps. 19:1, RSV). In verse 4 we read "In them he has set a tent for the sun." David heard thunder on the cedar-covered hills of Lebanon and it became the prayer that we call Psalm 29. "The voice of the LORD breaks the cedars, the LORD breaks the cedars of Lebanon" (v. 5, RSV).

The beauty of the bird's song; the majesty of the mountain and ocean; the fresh glories of daffodils in spring; the warm color of the maple leaves in October — these and a thousand other experiences can become part of our prayer life. John Gurney aptly expresses this theme in his hymn:

> Yes, God is good: in earth and sky,
> From ocean-depths and spreading wood,

Ten thousand voices seem to cry,
"God made us all, and God is good."

We hear it in the rushing breeze;
The hills that have for ages stood,
The echoing sky and roaring seas,
All swell the chorus, "God is good."

Recently, my daughter and I were admiring a herd of thoroughbred cattle and her student friend remarked, "I didn't know a cow could be beautiful."

To some, beauty of the seashore will be just that, while others may yet learn to see His glory in nature. If so, they will not merely have opened the windows of their lives to untold pleasures, but will also have entered a new dimension in the life of prayer.

### SEVEN: BIBLE READING

We so often hear the phrase "prayer and Bible reading" that it is apt to disguise the fact that if the Bible is rightly read it is a form of prayer in itself.

If we are in a small group of people and the conversation is dominated by one person, we do not normally regard it as satisfactory communication. Similarly, true prayer does not make God the target of a barrage of words. We need to listen as well as talk to Him. One of the best ways to listen to Him is to read His Word.

Psalm 1 tells us that the happy man is the one whose delight is in the law of the Lord, and on His law he meditates day and night. It goes on to explain that such a man is like a tree planted by streams of water, that yields its fruit in its season, and its leaf does not wither. The Arabs have a saying about a palm tree: "It likes its head in hell and its feet in water." In other words, however hot and dry may be the desert the tree will be a picture of freshness and fruitfulness, as long as its roots are in water. So it is with the man who is meditating upon the Word of God.

*     *     *

These are some of the facets of prayer. Let us be sure that we understand them and put them into operation. In practice we shall not want to split hairs about varieties of prayer. However, it is important to be aware of their existence.

# 4 Why Doesn't God Answer My Prayers?

When I was a young Christian it seemed that I often received the most dramatic answers to my prayers. This happens far less often today, and many of my friends admit the same thing, although most are slow to do so in public. In churches it is common to talk about the answers to prayer, but many people seem to think they should be quiet about the times God does not seem to answer. It is almost as if they feel they have to guard God's reputation.

When I first faced this problem I found that several well-meaning Christians would say, "God does answer. No is an answer." To me this always seemed to skate around the problem too easily to be convincing. For another, the Bible tells us to, "Ask what you will, and it shall be given you." "No" seems a poor answer to that.

I have found that the more honest and idealistic the person is, the bigger this problem is likely to be. The faith of some appears to have splintered under the impact of unanswered prayer.

Fortunately the Bible is not as afraid to talk about it as we are. The Bible is not only a book of answered prayers but also of unanswered prayers.

### ABRAHAM

There is an incident in the life of Abraham where he had a prayer refused and it is significant and instructive. It is recorded in Genesis 17. When God had first called Abraham to leave his home He promised the childless Abraham that he would have children and that his descendants would become "a great nation."

Abraham waited for eleven years and no child was born to him. There being no adoption agencies, Abraham followed the advice of Sarah, his wife, and produced a son named Ishmael by his wife's maid, named Hagar.

This introduces us to one of the greatest problems of prayer, that of the time factor. Abraham waited a long time, by our standards, and then tried to help God out. What he did not realize is that time in the plans of God is different from our timetables. "With the Lord one day is as a thousand years" (2 Peter 3:8, RSV). It may be easier for us to grasp this when we remember that one day on Venus is the equivalent of 200 of ours, on the moon one day is equivalent to thirty of ours and on Jupiter one day is the equivalent of ten hours on earth.

Once we grasp this we realize that God is outside the system into which we are locked. As A. W. Tozer has said, "God appears at the beginning of time and the end of time simultaneously." That is a hard concept to grasp.

The problem Abraham had with prayer was simply the question of time, and that is frequently our problem. God is never in a hurry but He is never late. He has already lived all our tomorrows.

After the birth of Ishmael to Abraham by Hagar, Ishmael became a firm favorite with Abraham. At the time of the incident we are considering he was thirteen years old, "all boy," and was the center of Abraham's affection. A great day occurred when God made a special appearance to Abraham to announce that He was about to enter into a new contract or covenant with him, and that part of the blessing God was going to give him was that in a matter of months, Sarah, his wife, would bear him a son.

There were two snags. First, Abraham was too fond of Ishmael to want any other child to take his place. Second, the age factor. Abraham was a hundred years old and Sarah was ninety. What is more, she had never been able to bear children. Abraham's first response was to laugh; the second to pray. What was his prayer? "O that Ishmael might live in thy sight" (Gen. 17:18, RSV). In other words his prayer was that instead

41

of another son, God would accept Ishmael as his heir.

The response of God to this prayer was immediate and to the point — No. "Sarah your wife shall bear you a son, and you shall call his name Isaac" (Gen. 17:19, RSV).

God refused to answer the prayer of Abraham for good reasons. First, God was going to prove that He was a miracle-working God. Second, He had specially chosen Abraham and Sarah as the originators of the stock that would become the nation of Israel. Third, He was a God who did not break His promises. He was a contract-keeping God.

Abraham's prayer did nothing to change the purposes of God because He had something far better in store for Abraham. The only thing the prayer did was to cloud a day bright with the sunshine of God's special appearance and of His special promise.

### THE DEMONIAC

There is an incident in the life of Jesus that is far more poignant and difficult to understand. It is in the fifth chapter of Mark and is the story of the man filled with demons. In the first twenty verses of that chapter three prayers are prayed to Jesus by three different people. Two were answered and one was refused. In many ways it seems to us that it was the one which was refused that should have been answered.

It is the story of the demoniac, a tormented

creature who was a threat to himself and to everyone else. He was an outcast from society. When Jesus appeared on the scene He quickly cast out the demons and healed the tortured creature, who was soon to be seen with Jesus, "sitting there clothed and in his right mind" (Mark 5:15, RSV).

The first prayer prayed that day was by the demons, who, when they knew that Jesus was about to cast them out of the man, asked Jesus to allow them to enter a herd of swine instead. Jesus answered the prayer.

The second prayer was prayed by the local inhabitants who were not comfortable with such miraculous doings. Their prayer to Jesus was that He would leave their locality. Jesus agreed to their prayer and made plans for immediate departure.

The third prayer was prayed by the man who had been healed by Jesus. He was filled with gratitude and love. He longed to know more about this wonderful person he had just met for the first time. Doubtless he wanted to serve Jesus. He begged to be allowed to travel with Him as He left, but Jesus refused his request and instructed him to go home.

The demons had their prayer answered, as did the inhospitable local inhabitants. The only prayer that sprang from true love and devotion was refused. Can you imagine how the healed man must have felt?

We can understand why this prayer was refused. Traveling away from home with Jesus he would merely be one in a crowd of disciples. Staying at home he was a living reminder of the power of Jesus. "And he went away and began to proclaim in the Decapolis how much Jesus had done for him; and all men marveled" (v. 20, RSV). To us now the refusal makes sense, but to the demoniac at the time it must have been a crushing blow.

## PAUL

Our next example is especially ironic. Paul was a man who had healed many people in answer to his prayers, but when he prayed for healing for himself, his prayers were ineffective. The account is in 2 Corinthians 12:7-10. We are not certain what Paul's physical ailment was, but there is good reason to believe it was connected with his sight. His ministry demanded continual travel and health was important. He was particularly called to minister to the Greeks who regarded physical perfection as important. Healing would not only spare him a great deal of suffering, but could make his ministry more effective, and would make him less dependent upon other people.

Three times Paul prayed for healing, but God refused it to him. Paul himself explains the reasons. First, it made him dependent upon God because he could not trust his own strength. Second, it kept him from being too proud at the wonderful revelations God had given him. Third, the fact that he was so marvelously used despite his physical limitations was a great testimony to the power of God. What Paul did not mention was that for centuries to come countless Christians struggling to serve Christ despite weakness and limitations would be inspired by this experience. They would learn with Paul, to "all the more gladly boast of my weaknesses, that the power of Christ may rest upon me" knowing that "when I am weak, then I am strong" (2 Cor. 12:9,10, RSV).

### JESUS CHRIST

Even the Son of God knew the experience of unanswered prayer. His prayer in the Garden of Gethsemane was so important to Him that He prayed it three times. Everything in Him recoiled from the ordeal of crucifixion that was just ahead. The physical sufferings themselves were barbaric, but far worse was the thought of the One who had never sinned, becoming sin for the sake of the world. Worst of all it would mean that He who had always known such intimate fellowship with the Father was to be deserted by Him; a fact that would cause to be wrung from His lips the phrase, "My God, my God, why hast Thou forsaken me?" Small wonder then that as He anticipated all this ahead of Him He would pray, "My Father, if it be possible, let this cup pass from me" (Matt. 26:39, RSV).

If that cup had been permitted to pass from Him, if the prayer had been answered, there would have been no salvation — no hope for mankind. Even as He prayed the prayer, He added "not as I will, but as thou wilt." The greatest blessing the world has ever known was God's refusal to answer Jesus' prayer to escape the cup.

It is not always possible for us to know at the time, why God does not answer our prayers, but there always is a good reason or reasons.

*    *    *

In eternity we shall all rejoice in the way we have known the Lord and the way He has answered our prayers, but then we shall be just as glad for the prayers He did not answer because then we shall see the complete picture.

# 5 Prayer in the Bible

This is not the place for an exhaustive treatment of the subject of the Bible and prayer. Many biblical principles of prayer have been mentioned in earlier chapters, but an overview of the place of prayer in the Bible is helpful.

Philosophy may be concerned with *ideas about* God; true religion is concerned with *communication with* God. In that sense the whole of the Bible is prayer-centered. It is concerned not merely with theories, but also with the fact of communication between God and man.

## OLD TESTAMENT

We are accustomed to thinking of Abraham as a man of prayer, but it is important to realize that prayer in one form or another occurred frequently long before the time of Abraham. Prayer is recorded in connection with Adam, even though some of it may appear to be negative in character. Consider a passage as early as Genesis 5 and what it reveals about Enoch. "Enoch walked with God; and he was not, for God took him" (v. 24, RSV). That this is an important and deliberate description is clear from the reference to it in the New Testament. "By faith Enoch was taken up so that he should not see death; and he was not found, because God had taken him" (Heb. 11:5, RSV).

Genesis 6 through 9 reveals that there was real communication between God and Noah, although the written word records far more of what God said to Noah than vice versa. So prayer continued in the lives of Abraham, Jacob, Joseph, and Moses — all are rich in examples of prayer in various forms and differing situations. Moses was a man of prayer and he always kept as his first priority the glory of God. His prayers in Exodus 32:11-13 and Joshua 7:9 show a great concern for God's reputation.

In the Book of Psalms we have literally a prayer book: prayers to music, prayers in Hebrew poetry, prayers of penitence (such as Ps. 51), prayers in the midst of suffering, prayers of faith and confidence, and glorious prayers of adoration (see list on page 29).

There are even prayers of cursing, e.g. Psalms 7; 52; 94. These usually were prayed by people like David in times of particular betrayal, suffering, and persecution. Some dismiss or disapprove of these psalms (as did C. S. Lewis in his

*Reflections on the Psalms*), but many a child of God under persecution has derived great comfort from them. They can provide a sorrowing Christian with the sense of kinship and reassurance that comes from knowing that someone else has passed through the same fires. Do not expect to understand them except under circumstances similar to the ones in which they were written. Note also that the psalmist's enemies are God's enemies; these are not purely personal grievances. The Psalms of cursing spring not only from personal anguish but also from distress and horror at what evil men are doing to God's people — the wolves are tearing the tender lambs. Psalm 52, for instance, was written when Doeg the Edomite committed the treachery which led to the deaths of all the Lord's priests at Nob. Similar examples are to be found in Psalms 35:1-8; 59; 109. The psalmist is praying not merely for his own vindication, but mainly expressing the longing that God's perfect justice will prevail. This is an essential emphasis for a perfect balance of truth. Nevertheless we should remember to bless, not curse our enemies.

In Isaiah 56:7 we read, "My house shall be called a house of prayer for all peoples" (RSV). In common with much of the prophetic literature this involves the combination of prophecy and prayer. Some prophetic writing may seem to be obscure, but there is much we can learn from it about prayer. A careful study of the prophecy of Jeremiah will provide examples. How often

Jeremiah longed to flee from spiritual conflict but was renewed constantly by his communication with God.

Consider the wealth of meaning in one short prayer of Elijah: "O LORD, God of Abraham, Isaac, and Israel, let it be known this day that thou art God in Israel, and that I am thy servant" (1 Kings 18:36, RSV). The whole of Elijah's ambition is revealed in this moment of personal crisis: "let it be known this day that thou art God." This prayer reveals his passion to see God vindicated and given His rightful place.

In James 5:16-18 we read, "The prayer of a righteous man has great power in its effects. Elijah was a man of like nature with ourselves and he prayed fervently that it might not rain, and for three years and six months it did not rain on the earth. Then he prayed again and the heaven gave rain" (RSV). It is important to emphasize that Elijah was not only a righteous man, but also had the right motive, and knew the purpose of God. A good treatment of this is in the book, *A Man Just Like Us*, by Harold W. Fife.

### IN EXILE

While the temple existed it was the center of worship. Temple worship followed the form that came from God through Moses. Its distinctive features were: 1) a particular building in a central location; 2) a special priesthood; 3) sacrifice and ritual ceremonies. When the temple was destroyed and the Jews went into exile, their faith had to find other expression; it did so through the growth of synagogue worship. Whereas the center of temple worship was priests and blood sacrifice, the center of synagogue worship was the reading of Scripture, prayer, and exposition.

This synagogue worship became so highly regarded that even when the temple was rebuilt, first under Zerubbabel and then under Herod, the synagogue worship still flourished. There are many instances in the life of Jesus Christ when He attended the synagogue. It is obvious from Acts 6:9: "Then some of those who belonged to the synagogue of the Freedmen (as it was called), and of the Cyrenians, and of the Alexandrians, and of those from Cilicia and Asia, arose and disputed with Stephen," (RSV), that in the early apostolic church synagogue worship played an important role even in Jerusalem, almost in the shadow of the temple.

Many Christians seem ignorant about synagogue worship. This is unfortunate because the early church soon took on the flavor more of the synagogue than of the temple. Blood sacrifice had been outmoded with the sacrifice of Jesus, "He has no need, like those high priests, to offer sacrifices daily, first for his own sins and then for those of the people: he did this once for all when he offered up himself" (Heb. 7:27, RSV). The emphasis on prayer and Bible teaching, and the location of many churches in scattered communities, also contributed to making the church more similar to the synagogue than to the temple. One of the most helpful books in describing what all this means to the modern practicing Jew is Herman Wouk's book, *This is my God*, published by Doubleday & Co.

Perhaps the easiest way to discover the place of prayer in the apostolic church is simply to take a concordance, look up the word "prayer" and see how frequent is its use from Acts 2 to the end of the New Testament. The reading of Acts also, and the noting of each reference to prayer, is challenging and inspiring.

There are constant reminders that the early church was conceived in prayer, and that prayer, together with teaching, was the first priority of the apostles and the church. "We will devote ourselves to prayer and to the ministry of the Word" (Acts 6:4, RSV).

When Ananias was commissioned to go to Paul and lay hands on him after his conversion, the change in Paul was described as "he is praying" (Acts 9:11, RSV).

\*　　\*　　\*

In Paul's letters he frequently mentions how often he prays for those to whom he writes, and urges them to pray for others, too. Prayer gushes out of Paul like living springs, even in the middle of a paragraph. Sometimes he prays that his readers will have love, or wise judgment, and be Christlike, but often he is just overflowing with prayers and benedictions expressing his love and adoration for the Lord.

# 6 Does Prayer Change Things?

Many Christians have a motto: "Prayer Changes Things." This motto, among others, is often repeated at prayer meetings and also in private conversations. But does prayer change things? Many Christians hold a deep conviction that it does. Many others, just as sincere and well-taught would question this.

As soon as we raise this matter we are faced with two extreme points of view. Each has an element of truth in it, but each also contains the seeds of danger and even disaster. The first of these extremes suggests that prayer is a power that compels God to comply with our wishes. This attitude undercuts the sovereignty of God and implies that He can be manipulated by man.

The other extreme is to think of God as a power pursuing an undeviating course that nothing can modify. This makes men into pawns and is close to complete fatalism, which is more truly characteristic of Islam than Christianity. I do not wish to split hairs, but we are not going to be able to think accurately about prayer unless we are precise in our terms.

Whatever may be the common view on the subject, prayer does not change things. The Bible teaches that prayer influences God who sometimes changes things. There are three assertions we must make on the subject of whether prayer changes things.

### THINGS ARE SOMETIMES CHANGED BY GOD AS A RESULT OF PRAYER

A number of Scriptures support this assertion.

*Abraham* — Genesis 18:22,23. This passage makes it clear that in response to the prayer of Abraham, God agreed not to bring judgment upon Sodom if ten righteous people could be found in the city. There were not ten righteous people and Sodom was destroyed, but the possibility of God influencing events in answer to prayer is established. It is also important to note that God had foreknowledge of the events described.

*Moses* — Exodus 32:9-14. This chapter narrates an experience that occurred during the Israelites' wanderings in the wilderness. Moses left his people camped at the foot of Mount Sinai and climbed the mountain for special fellowship with God. He was gone almost six weeks, and the

Israelites became impatient and gave him up for lost. They rejected God; they built a calf of gold, made it an instant God, and worshiped it. "And the LORD said to Moses, 'I have seen this people, and behold, it is a stiffnecked people; now therefore let me alone, that my wrath may burn hot against them and I may consume them; but of you I will make a great nation. But Moses besought the LORD his God and said, 'O LORD, why does thy wrath burn hot against thy people, whom thou hast brought forth out of Egypt with great power and with a mighty hand?. . . .' And the LORD repented of the evil which he thought to do to his people" (vv. 9-11,14, RSV). This is another prayer pregnant with meaning, but note just two facts. First, it was God's reputation that concerned Moses, as we see in verse 12. Second, God modified His announced intention as a result of Moses' prayer.

I referred in chapter 5 to the incident when God caused a drought in answer to Elijah's prayer. Of course there are also many examples of answers to prayer in the New Testament. These occur not merely in the life of Jesus but also in the early church, e.g. Acts 12:5. "So Peter was kept in prison; but earnest prayer for him was made to God by the church" (RSV). The sequel was that Peter was miraculously released from prison. The clear implication is that the miracle was related to the prayer of the church. There are of course many more examples in Scripture and in present-day experience.

The second assertion is almost more important because it is so seldom talked and written about.

### THINGS ARE NOT ALWAYS CHANGED AS A RESULT OF PRAYER

The whole matter of unanswered prayer was dealt with more thoroughly in chapters 4 and 5. We must repeat, however, that there were occasions when the prayers of such spiritual giants as Abraham, Moses, Paul, and even Jesus Christ were unanswered. We should learn from their experiences.

Our views on prayer must not be based upon wishful thinking, nor upon the testimony of Christians, but upon the teaching of the Word of God.

### GOD CHANGES PEOPLE WHO PRAY

Superficially, the most wonderful thing about prayer may seem to be that as a result of it circumstances can be changed. In fact, a much more wonderful and important fact is that through prayer the person who prays is changed. I learned that instead of praying "Lord, please help me find a parking place," it was better to pray "Help me to find a parking place or give me patience to walk a few blocks." Actually for me, the second part was the greater miracle.

The most dramatic illustration of the change in a man caused by prayer is that of Moses. "Moses did not know that the skin of his face shone because he had been talking with God"

(Exod. 34:29, RSV). No wonder the following verses describe the fear and wonder of Aaron and the people when they saw something of God's glory reflected in the face of Moses. Moses is the most dramatic example of the fact that people who spend much time with God begin to share His likeness. This is surely what Paul meant when he wrote that "we all, with unveiled face, beholding the glory of the Lord, are being changed into His likeness from one degree of glory to another" (2 Cor. 3:18, RSV).

*   *   *

Paul wrote in Romans 8:29 that "Those whom he foreknew he also predestined to be conformed to the image of his Son" (RSV). The will of God for His children is not necessarily that they be successful, but that they become like Jesus Christ. This process of change will not take place unless we exercise prayer in its widest and fullest sense.

# 7 Prayer in the Life of Our Lord

It would not be difficult to fill an entire book with a discussion of prayer in the life of our Lord, but we shall consider only three incidents here.

## THE IMPORTANCE OF PRAYER (MARK 1)

Throughout the life of our Lord we read repeatedly that He retired from the company of people to seek solitude for prayer. For this purpose He climbed mountains and traveled into deserts. To get a complete picture of this we need to examine the events of one crowded day in the life of Christ as it is recorded in Mark 1:21-38. In these verses we learn that at the beginning of the day He went to the synagogue and taught. At the conclusion of His sermon He was confronted with a man who was demon possessed. The demon yielded to our Lord's authority and was cast out.

Immediately after this incident He sought rest and refreshment in the house of Simon (v.29). Upon entering the home He was told that Peter's mother-in-law was sick with a fever, so He healed her.

There seems to be an unspoken assumption that for Jesus, preaching, counseling, healing, and exorcism were effortless. Careful reading of His life story would indicate that the reverse was true. He was not only perfect deity but also human. When the disciples were energetic enough to sail in a boat in a fierce storm Jesus slept the sleep of exhaustion and was in perfect peace as He slept on the floor of the boat (Mark 4:37,38). In John's gospel we read that in the course of traveling "Jesus, wearied as he was with his journey, sat down" (John 4:6, RSV). while His disciples still had strength and energy to walk into the city to buy food.

If we think that we alone know the mind-numbing effects of fatigue — physical, mental, and spiritual — let us remind ourselves that we have "one who in every respect has been tempted as we are" (Heb. 4:15, RSV), and that obviously included exhaustion.

A further illustration of the exhausting nature of the ministry of Jesus Christ is recorded in Mark 5:25-30. He was in the midst of a great crowd, and among those who thronged about Him was a woman who had suffered from hemorrhages for twelve years. Her faith was such that she believed if only she could touch

His garment she would be healed. She touched and she was healed. Jesus then asked who had touched Him. The disciples were astonished and said to Him, "You see the crowd pressing around you, and yet you say, 'Who touched me?' " Jesus asked this question because "Jesus [perceived] in himself that power had gone forth from him" (v. 30, RSV).

These incidents are a clear evidence that Jesus paid a physical and emotional price whenever He engaged in ministry to man.

When Isaiah wrote prophetically, "Surely he has borne our griefs and carried our sorrows" (Isa. 53:4, RSV), he was referring not only to the great fact of Calvary but also to the life of our Lord from the cradle to the empty tomb.

With this in mind let us go back to the incidents of the Sabbath day recorded in Mark's gospel. After preaching, casting out a demon, and healing the mother-in-law of Peter, Jesus had had little rest: "That evening, at sundown, they brought to him all who were sick or possessed with demons. And the whole city was gathered together about the door. And he healed many who were sick with various diseases, and cast out many demons" (1:32-34, RSV). Have you ever felt so weary that you were numb with fatigue? Think how Jesus felt as He eventually laid Himself down to sleep. Surely He deserved to sleep late!

This was not to be, for we go on to read in verse 35, "And in the morning, a great while before day, he rose and went out to a lonely place, and there he prayed'' (RSV). It was years ago that the implication of this hit me like a sledge hammer: *prayer was for Jesus more important than sleep.* I was eventually to learn that this does not mean we should neglect our sleep. My wife once asked me, ''Do you really think that you are glorifying God by dragging yourself around half dead?'' The first lesson to be learned is not that sleep is less necessary than prayer, but that each is indispensible, as are both wings of an airplane.

The deepest significance of this incident did not dawn on me for many years. It is found in the next two verses, ''And Simon and those who were with him pursued him, and they found him and said to him, 'Every one is searching for you''' (vv. 36,37, RSV). What a wonderful opportunity for ministry was lost because Jesus was alone in prayer! Jesus' reply to the news that people were seeking Him is striking: ''Let us go on to the next towns . . .'' (v. 38, RSV).

For me the most important lesson to learn, but the hardest to practice, is not merely that prayer is more important than sleep, but that *prayer is more important than Christian service.*

### PRIORITIES IN PRAYER (MATT. 6)

What has become known as ''The Lord's Prayer'' is found in Matthew 6:9-13. In some ways the title is unfortunate as other passages of Scripture could more accurately be so described.

It is really the "Disciples' Prayer" as taught by our Lord, and is but a fragment of the glorious body of truth in the Sermon on the Mount.

In this chapter Jesus warns the disciples of the danger of praying to impress men rather than God (v. 5), and of merely heaping up empty phrases (v. 7).

Then the prayer begins with an introduction — "Our Father who art in heaven." This establishes our relationship. "Father" speaks of intimacy, and "heaven" reminds us of His deity. Following this we have the next seven phrases:

1. "Hallowed be thy name"
2. "Thy kingdom come"
3. "Thy will be done, on earth as it is in heaven"
4. "Give us this day our daily bread"
5. "And forgive us our debts"
6. "Lead us not into temptation"
7. "But deliver us from evil."

We notice in this model prayer that the first three requests are concerned with the glory of God, His name, and His kingdom. This is a good example for us to follow. The fourth request is for our daily temporal needs. Requests 5, 6, and 7 are concerned with personal forgiveness and deliverance from evil and temptation. To summarize, the first three requests are concerned with God and His glory. The last three are concerned with our spiritual needs, and the central one is concerned with our physical and material needs. All this follows the glorious promise, "your Father knows what you need" (v. 8).

We see clearly the importance of prayer in the first chapter of Mark. In Matthew 6 we learn what should be the order of priorities in our prayer time.

### THE HIGH PRIESTLY PRAYER (JOHN 17)

The New Testament frequently records the fact that Jesus prayed but rarely tells us how He prayed, or for what. This passage in John 17 comes after the desertion by Judas Iscariot and before our Lord's crucifixion. It is unique and is regarded by many as being one of the richest passages in the New Testament.

The account John gives of this prayer is so detailed, it seems to indicate either that he took recorded notes, or, more likely, he was so impressed by it that he spoke about it often and so kept it fresh in his memory. This chapter has received great attention from men who were great in scholarship and godliness. Our purpose here is not to be exhaustive or original, but to emphasize a few truths that are revealed in this unique insight into our Lord Jesus in prayer.

*The Paradox* (vv. 1-5). At the outset of the prayer reference is made to the impending death of Christ, but the way in which Jesus refers to it makes it clear that while to men such an event could only be disastrous, to our Lord it was glorious.

The turning of tragedy into triumph becomes evident throughout the prayer of Jesus. Death is not the end of hope, but is indeed the gateway to life. This great paradox had already been explained by Jesus many times, and recently in John 12:23-33. It was never understood by His disciples until after Pentecost. Later this paradox is repeatedly expounded by Paul and the other apostles. "The cross is the glory of God because self sacrifice is the expression of love," wrote William Temple.

"I have manifested thy name to the men whom thou gavest me out of the world" (v. 6, RSV). This was a matter that puzzled Judas (not Iscariot) for in John 14:22 he asked Jesus, "Lord, how is it that you will manifest yourself to us, and not to the world?" (RSV). The question is a perennial one and the answer is implicit in this reply of Jesus. "I do not pray that thou shouldest take them out of the world" (John 17:15, RSV). Jesus was to leave the world (v. 11) but His disciples were to stay. They were to be His presence and His ambassadors. That is why He manifested His glory to them. There is no room in the New Testament for the monastery. The old converted slave driver John Newton commented, "The world is the place where we bring glory to the Lord," and he knew better than most the wickedness of the world and the glory of his God.

Our Lord's birth, His life, His miracles, His teaching — all revealed His deity, but His glory was manifested only to His disciples. The ordinary pagan enjoys the water being turned into wine: the believer sees beyond the sign and sees the glory of the Father manifested. It is ever so. Every picture tells a story, but some see only the paint. To be His ambassadors — His presence in a world that disowned Him, and sent Him to a humiliating death — what a task and what a privilege! How does He pray for His disciples in their new role?

*Unity* (vv. 21-23). "That they may all be one; even as thou, Father, art in me, and I in thee, that they also may be in us, so that the world may believe . . ." (RSV). The unity of believers with each other is no less than an extension of the unity of the godhead. The spirit of the world is disintegration. The Spirit of the Lord is oneness.

*Kept* (v. 15). "I . . . pray that thou shouldest . . . keep them from the evil one" (RSV). A part of that keeping process is the power of truth. "Sanctify them in the truth; thy word is truth" (v. 17, RSV). The word sanctify can mislead. It sometimes is translated as purity, but that is inadequate. Purity is infinitely good but it is a negative quality. Our Lord is praying that they may be positively holy through the ministry of His truth.

*Joy* (v. 13). "That they may have my joy fulfilled in themselves" (RSV). Someone recently described a certain group of Christians by saying, "they neither love nor laugh." What an indictment if it is true. Christian faith that lacks compassion and laughter is like a fireplace without a fire, or a reading lamp without a bulb.

\*    \*    \*

So in these three episodes in the life of Jesus we see the importance of prayer, the priorities in prayer, and are reminded that we are the people for whom He lives to make intercession.

# 8 Prayer in Practice

To read this chapter without first reading the preceding chapters would inevitably lead to the reader being misinformed and the writer being misunderstood. What appears in the next few pages is written on the assumption that we know the conditions of prayer, some of the varieties of prayer, why some prayers are unanswered, the place of prayer in the life of our Lord, and so on. For instance, if we do not pray with a right motive, prayer will be an exercise in futility.

Concerning putting prayer into practice it will be convenient to give some practical advice under two separate headings. First, on a personal basis; second, in a group situation.

### PERSONAL PRAYER

*Individuality and prayer.* We are not robots or even "souls"; we are children of God. Each child has his own personality, weaknesses, and strengths. The Good Shepherd knows each of His sheep and calls him by his name.

Beware whom you imitate. It is right to regard the apostle Paul as an example, but wrong to regard Hudson Taylor as one to be slavishly imitated. What was good and right for him may be undesirable for us.

It has been stressed that true prayer has many facets, and that it really consists of a total relationship between God and His children. Each Christian is an individual with different characteristics and his or her prayer life will reflect these individualities. I have three children. My love for them is equal, but because they are separate individuals with different personalities and varying degrees of expression, the type and frequency of my communication with them will be different. Your prayer life should not be a carbon copy of the prayer life of another Christian. It has taken me many years to shake off the bondage of that which is mere tradition, and separate it from that which is biblical and therefore authoritative.

Be natural in prayer. God hates phonies. Queen Victoria used to say that one of the things she disliked about Prime Minister Gladstone was "that he always addressed me as if I were a public meeting!"

Some people have stunted their prayer lives by giving undue importance to the position and attitude of the body. One of my friends used to advise Christians not only to have a prayer time each morning, but also to get washed and dressed first so they could bring to it an attitude of efficiency and respect. That sort of advice may help some people, but Jesus' emphasis was that we should worship God in spirit and in truth. He did not specify that we should be dressed formally.

One sincere Christian I know has a strong conviction that he should always stand to pray. Since he is tall it can be quite disconcerting when he is praying in a small group. He suddenly jumps to his feet and begins to address God at least three feet above the heads of his friends.

It is not necessary to stand, kneel, hold hands, or shut our eyes to pray. Some of these techniques may help to discourage wandering thoughts, and if so, then by all means use them, but do not be a slave to them. Never postpone praying until you can find a suitable place and atmosphere — it may never come. A great writer once said, "To the Christian, every bush is a burning bush and all ground is holy ground, every day is a holy day." You can address God wherever you happen to be; He is there, too.

Freedom must not be an excuse for sloppiness, however. I suppose it is possible for a person to become a mature and well-taught Christian without being disciplined and systematic about his devotional life — but I have never met such a person.

The Bible doesn't indicate how long a period each Christian should spend in devotions each day. The Christian life is not taught and lived by strict regulations. However, the New Testament writers do stress that Bible knowledge is important, as is every type of prayer. I have seen many jellyfish Christians become stable men and women of God after putting into practice the teaching of *The Quiet Time*, a classic book on a life of personal devotion published by InterVarsity Press.

Cultivate the attitude of relating every experience to God. Beauty, joy, sadness, sickness, need, failure, and successes — nothing in our experience is irrelevant to Him. Christ has been through it all Himself. We have much in common and it is only natural that we should talk it over with Him.

### SYSTEMATIC PRAYER

Almost every conceivable system for use in personal prayer has been advocated at one time or another. Most of them are of some help to some Christians at some time, but some of them cause more problems than they solve.

I have used most systems of prayer at some time in my life. For example, I have made use of fairly elaborate prayer lists. I have allocated a certain period of time each day. At one stage I resolved to stay on my knees in prayer for thirty minutes daily — even used a watch to time myself. As prayer it may have been of little value but my motive was good, and a small element of self-sacrifice was involved. It certainly did no harm, so why fret? What is good in one stage of life may not be best for another stage.

Even the metabolism of our body has its influence on our prayer life. Some people are most alert early in the morning, others later on. The busy housewife may find that the best time for prayer is when the children have left for school. Use your intelligence to decide what is the time a) when you are most alert, and b) when you are least likely to be interrupted. If it means taking the telephone off the hook for thirty minutes, do that. Some have found that time spent in commuting to work can be used profitably in this way.

By all means find a good system and use it, but beware lest your system leads you to a mechanical attitude to prayer, for that can damage and destroy the spontaneity which should be an element in all relationships.

One godly and systematic man I knew once advised me on how to take care of my family relationships. He suggested that I set aside Sunday afternoons for this, allocating one hour to my wife and half an hour each to my children. The period I spent with each person should be divided fifty-fifty between talking and listening. Evidently the system was helpful to him and to his family. Knowing myself and my family I knew such a system would have reduced them or me to frustration or even insanity.

We have to decide for ourselves whether our prayer life will be systematically catalogued or whether it will be a matter of relating each experience and need to God as it arises. It probably should contain an element of each. There are two extremes into which it is easy to fall and which should be avoided. Too systematic an approach to prayer can fossilize our prayer lives, and can produce a guilt complex if, for any reason, our system is disrupted. On the other hand, too much "freedom" tends to encourage a vague and haphazard prayer life, and sometimes no prayer life at all. If we want to have a vigorous relationship with God, we must learn to combine freedom with discipline.

In all personal prayer it is important to cultivate an attitude of repentance. Humility does not consist of thinking badly of yourself, but in not thinking at all of yourself. This does not involve morbidity or a change of personality. God does not change our personality . . . psychologists can and do. If you have an aggressive temperament God will need to discipline and refine it, but He does not change personality.

Another important part of personal prayer is Bible reading. One of the greatest developments in my spiritual life came when I formed the custom of reading through the Bible each year. After a dozen or so years I found it helpful to change this habit but it had provided a wonderful basis for life and faith. I expect I will eventually return to it.

The custom of giving thanks before eating is a useful illustration of the bewildering variety of customs common among various countries and within certain groups within some of those countries. In Britain table grace is usually brief and often formal. In the United States it is generally longer and the prayer can cover many subjects while the food grows cold and the cook becomes frustrated! Some groups pray before and after each meal. Quakers and others often pray silently; some sing grace, and so on.

Jesus Christ Himself is recorded as giving thanks before eating. However, some of these occasions were special and even of ritual significance, such as the Last Supper and the breaking of bread at Emmaus. There were a number of occasions when Jesus is not recorded as giving thanks, e.g. "Jesus came and took the bread and gave it to them, and so with the fish" (John 21:13, RSV).

One obvious fact is that we should be thankful; "do everything in the name of the Lord Jesus, giving thanks to God the Father through him" (Col. 3:17, RSV). What is not so obvious is the form or frequency the giving of thanks should have.

The purpose of giving thanks at meals, however, is often misunderstood. It is sometimes regarded primarily as a means of witness. If we "say grace" in public it will somehow be of benefit to unbelievers who may be present. The unspoken but largely accepted belief seems to be that the more obtrusive the "grace" the better. I was one of a party of perhaps twenty eating in a restaurant which seated about fifty, when the leader of the group decided that the best way to give thanks was to sing an appropriate grace. This we did, but in looking back I find it hard to believe that it favorably impressed the rest of the guests who would have included unbelievers, Jews, and possibly even Muslims.

The habit of praying so that all can observe puts us in dangerous company with the Pharisees, "Beware of practicing your piety before men in order to be seen by them" (Matt. 6:1, RSV). There are times when making a show of table prayers can be an intrusion and an embarrassment to non-Christians in a group. Those living in non-Christian homes must give thought to this. One friend of mine was convinced that thanksgiving for food should be confined to his private devotions. At the time, I disagreed, but on reflection I believe I was in the wrong. Too much rigidity of custom added to confusion of purpose can certainly destroy the spontaneity of prayer, and even deny God the true gratitude His provision deserves.

### GROUP PRAYER

Praying in a group situation, whether it be a small or a large group, can be an inspiring experience. Unfortunately, it more often tends to be a depressing one. It is probable that more so-called "white lies" are told in prayer than in almost any other situation.

Let us beware of being dogmatic about trivialities in our group; for instance, whether we use "thee and thou," "you and your," or a mixture of both forms. Language is always changing, and it is to be expected that these changes will be expressed in our prayer life.

It was in the last century that a daily newspaper carried an account of one Christian meeting. The article included the clever but sarcastic observation that "never was a more eloquent prayer offered to a Boston congregation." Unfortunately group prayer is still sometimes offered to the congregation rather than to the Lord God.

Group prayer can be simple and intimate. Consider the words of Malachi, "Then those who feared the LORD spoke with one another; the LORD heeded and heard them, and a book of remembrance was written before him of those who feared the LORD and thought on his name" (Mal. 3:16, RSV). The passage does not imply that the all-knowing God needed to have His memory stirred, but rather that God treasured the God-centered conversation of His children. We need to note two things about this: First, godly conversation is close to prayer and perhaps is in itself a form of prayer. Second, we need to ask ourselves how often our conversation achieves this standard.

Group prayer is almost a standing invitation for fads and gimmicks. Some years ago I was responsible for a weekly prayer meeting of approximately thirty people. I soon concluded that it was as dead a meeting as any I had attended. I tried every device I could over a period of six months. I arranged the seating in circles rather than rows; I persuaded people to pray briefer prayers; I tried to limit attendance to teenagers only; I chose the kind of music that would induce a "suitable atmosphere." At the end of six months I was beaten and I knew it. Gimmicks were not the answer.

I knew then that if that meeting was going to live, it would have to be the work of God Himself. He began to deal with us one by one, and the prayer meeting became the high point of each week. If prayer is to have life, the people praying need to be living.

I believe my first charismatic prayer meeting was in El Salvador, Central America. The pastor called for prayer and everyone began to speak at once. To me it seemed like bedlam, and I later told a missionary so. He smiled and explained. "These Christians get up at dawn, and they work all day in the fields in a hot, humid climate. When they come to an evening meeting they are close to exhaustion. If one person led in prayer for ten minutes many would fall asleep." Then he asked me, "Do you think that God is capable of hearing more than one person at a time?" Almost reluctantly I admitted He was. Eventually God used my Latin brothers to show me that many of my "convictions" about prayer were in fact Anglo-Saxon prejudices.

Conversational prayer, as the term implies, is a type of prayer which follows the form of group conversation. Most prayers are very brief. A phrase of a prayer by one person reminds another person to pray for a different aspect of the same topic and so it flows on. Let me give you an example of how it works:

A. "Lord, we pray for Virginia Slade in the hospital and ask that she might know your power of healing and peace."

B. "I would also pray for her husband that through this experience he might be drawn to Yourself."

C. "We pray too about his job situation, and in some way help him to know that we care and that You care even more than we do."

A. "Lord, we ask You to guide the doctors and nurses and may they be blessed through Virginia's life and witness."

D. "We are glad that their son John is now a believer and we ask You to help him to grow spiritually, and be a help to Jimmy and Sam."

E. "O Lord Jesus, it is so wonderful to know that You are more concerned about the Slade family than we are."

One of the disadvantages of conversational

prayer is that it can be difficult to tell whether or not a person has finished praying as the prayers are not concluded with an "Amen." The familiar atmosphere can lead to a lack of reverence. This way of praying will not suit all temperaments or even all nationalities. Do not try to force it upon people who are not ready for it.

There are, however, several advantages to conversational prayer. It is easier for a young Christian to start to pray in public in this more relaxed atmosphere. More people take part as the prayers are brief, which in turn makes it harder for peoples' minds to wander. It also is more conducive to sincerity because the prayers tend to flow naturally from each other rather than being thought out beforehand as set speeches. It also is true that "prayer cliches" are less likely to be used.

Like anything else, conversational prayer has its weaknesses but some of the most blessed times of prayer I have known have been conversational. This subject has been thoroughly covered by Rosalind Rinker in her book, *Prayer — Conversing With God*, published by Zondervan.

### PRAYER IN SUNDAY SERVICES

There are three main complications in dealing with this subject. First, the variety of practice in different countries, such as the United States, Latin America, and Great Britain. Second, the variation that exists within these countries. In the United States there is a wide range from the Baptists to the Episcopalians, and in Great Britain there are Episcopalian (Anglican), Independent and Brethren churches. Third, great changes currently are taking place in most countries and in most churches. The most dramatic illustration, after many centuries of custom, is the abolition of the use of Latin in Roman Catholic churches. In the Episcopalian churches in England there are various experiments now being carried out in the services and liturgy. Strangely enough there seems to be less flexibility and change in groups that for many years have rejected the liturgical forms of service and have prided themselves on flexibility. Their spontaneity sometimes has become as contrived as a carefully choreographed ballet.

There are at least two advantages of a liturgical service. They usually do justice to various types of prayer that otherwise are often neglected, such as confession and adoration, and for many Christians the liturgical service is a useful aid to worship.

There also are weaknesses. Many Christians comment on the beautiful phrasing of these printed prayers and that they produce an attitude of worship. It is possible to be emotionally moved by literature and music, by what we hear and see. The feeling may not necessarily be spiritual however; it may be aesthetic. The same feeling can be experienced in a concert hall.

The second problem I have with liturgical services, and I have participated in them hundreds of times (sometimes at their worst and other times at their best), is that I have never been able to rid myself of the feeling there is an element of the mechanical in them.

The third problem I have, is that the New Testament provides little authority for them.

For a period of years I have been responsible for leading the same congregation in at least three services a week, and I have found it a problem to preserve freshness and variety in public prayer. I have worshiped in churches where the pastor prayed for twenty minutes and I have occasionally dozed off — as have others when I have been leading a service!

It is vital to establish the nature of the role of prayer in a worship service. The New Testament clearly indicates that a major part of church life should be teaching and evangelism, but unfortunately that can lead to a situation in which everything else is regarded as "preliminaries"! In a real sense every part of the service is a type of prayer — including the offering and the sermon. The ideal prayer should normally include not only, nor even mainly, intercession and petition, but also adoration and confession.

I once was worshiping in a church in a Chicago suburb when after the pastor had prayed there was a pause, and he said, "I am not proud of that prayer. It was full of our needs and wants and not much concerned with confession or the glory of God." The atmosphere became almost electric. For me the experience confirmed a conviction I already had, namely that the pastor was a man of rare honesty and godliness — a rare specimen indeed.

The place of hymns as a form of prayer in public worship is grossly neglected. As I have suggested elsewhere in this book, a good hymnal rightly used will supply an important part of the prayer of believers. Hymns on God in Creation; Worship and Adoration; Penitence; etc., should normally be part of group prayer. There is in some circles in the church in the United States a growing emphasis on the importance of hymnody in worship. So far it does not seem to have penetrated far beyond certain Christian colleges, seminaries and magazines. In Great Britain the churches use a much greater number of hymns in most services and a larger range of hymns are in use. Outside of the Anglican Church there is little emphasis on "special music" but far more emphasis on congregational singing. More Christians in Great Britain seem to make hymnody a "hobby." The over-all effect may well be that the standard of music is higher in the church in the U.S.A. Congregational singing is often better in Great Britain, however, and hymns are more often used as a form of congregational prayer. The two emphases need not be mutually exclusive.

At one time, to give leadership in prayer and to preserve freshness, I used notes for my pulpit prayers. Perhaps that is what they became, more pulpit than prayer!

\*     \*     \*

In a small church situation where believers are spiritually alive I have discovered that an "open time for worship" and sometimes an "open time for intercession, etc." is perhaps the most exciting and creative type of group prayer. In a larger congregation a different situation exists. For most people, to sit in a relaxed physical position with eyes closed during the time, listening to one voice, is more likely to be used in sleep than in prayer. I would advocate having several mature people leading in brief prayers, covering some of the varieties of prayer that have been mentioned.

# 9 Pray As If

In our prayers we often aim at nothing and hit it every time. We expect nothing from God and get precisely that. Much of our praying never goes beyond the ceiling.

If we believe that God is as great as the Bible says He is, then nothing is beyond His power. If we believe He is vitally concerned with us and with His work, then we should pray as if He is not reluctant to bless but wanting to bless; not as if we are wringing blessings out of a reluctant God but as if we are talking over our circumstances with a Father who is able and longing to help us. Here are some suggestions for our praying.

*Pray As if God Can Do the Impossible*

It is possible to limit God by our own lack of confidence in Him. He can cure brain cancer. He can open prison doors. He can raise the dead. He can cure alcoholics. He can change a stubborn nature. He can help us do the impossible. "By thee I can crush a troop; and by my God I can leap over a wall" (Ps. 18:29, RSV).

## Pray As if God Knows Best

We know that God can work miracles, but we dare not try to use prayer to manipulate Him. We do not know enough to demand anything from God. Even Jesus prayed "Not my will, but thine be done." We rejoice that there is literally nothing beyond His control, but we acknowledge that as our heavenly Father He knows best.

## Pray As if Prayer Is Important

We frequently sing and say that prayer is important. Then it should occupy some of our time. Do we act as if it is vital? Pray as if prayer were a significant part of every day — at least as important as eating. Prayer is not optional; neither is it a necessary interruption to be completed as quickly as possible.

## Pray As if You Believe in God

Some people apparently believe that "Please God, bless the missionaries, the pastor, and mommy and daddy," is an adequate prayer. Such prayer is not only childish, but also reveals an ignorance of God, of other people, and of prayer itself.

If Christians honestly expect God to answer prayer, then their prayer will reflect their confidence in Him as a person. God is pleased with His children's belief; He is insulted by unbelief. "Whatever does not proceed from faith is sin" (Rom. 14:23, RSV).

## Pray As if You Were Using Your Intelligence

God is not in need of information, but we are. God gave us a mind, therefore we must use it. We must not leave our minds outside our prayer life. If we believe that prayer is related to a proper understanding of God, we should take trouble to be sure that our ideas about God are accurate.

If we believe that just asking God to "bless" people is inadequate, then we have to do something about learning about their specific needs. If we think God is concerned with other Christian's material problems, we must act as if He is, and get information about them. If God is interested in our friends' health or in their difficulties at work, we should find out about these things.

How can we get information about missionaries, so as to pray for them intelligently? Probably only by establishing fairly intimate correspondence with one or two of them. We should ask them to take us into their confidence, and assure them of our personal concern.

If we think God is concerned about thermonuclear warfare, then we must pray as if it is important to know something of world affairs. A good newspaper or news magazine may make a contribution to our prayer life. We are to read them to sharpen our awareness of world trends, geographic locations, and political as well as religious events.

*Pray As if the People You Pray for Are Human*

If we are sometimes irritable, if we haven't had enough sleep, are sick of the rain, or tired of the heat, our friends and neighbors are, too. If we need God's correction and maturing, we should pray for this in the life of church leaders as well. Crossing a body of water doesn't transform the missionary into a supernatural spiritual being, always capable and always on top. We should pray for an extra allowance of strength, wisdom, and patience for them.

Have you ever crammed for exams, knowing your need of God's help in your study? The missionary is learning a foreign language under none-too-perfect study conditions.

If you would like to throw in the sponge, remember that your pastor may also be meeting a crisis that makes him long for an easier life. If you find prayer time next to impossible, think of the business executive in your church — he often brings his work home with him at the same time he is trying to raise a family. If you are frustrated, discouraged, or depressed, remember that Satan doesn't reserve temptations for you alone.

*Pray As if People Depended on Your Prayers*

If you need someone you can trust to pray for you, then your friends do, too. Pray as if they are your responsibility. Allow the Holy Spirit to find a sensitive and responsive heart in you for their needs.

\*  \*  \*

"Pray at all times with every kind of spiritual prayer, keeping alert and persistent as you pray for all Christ's men and women" (Eph. 6:18, Phillips).